ideals® VALENTINE

More Than 50 Years of Celebrating Life's Most Treasured Moments

Vol. 53, No. 1

*"There is no surprise more magical
than the surprise of being loved."*
—*Charles Morgan*

IDEALS—Vol. 53, No. 1 February MCMXCVI IDEALS (ISSN 0019-137X) is published eight times a year:
February, March, May, June, August, September, November, December
by IDEALS PUBLICATIONS INCORPORATED, 535 Metroplex Drive, Suite 250, Nashville, TN 37211.
Second-class postage paid at Nashville, Tennessee, and additional mailing offices. Copyright © MCMXCVI by IDEALS PUBLICATIONS
INCORPORATED. POSTMASTER: Send address changes to Ideals, PO Box 305300, Nashville, TN 37230. All rights reserved.
Title IDEALS registered U.S. Patent Office.

SINGLE ISSUE—U.S. $5.95 USD; Higher in Canada
ONE-YEAR SUBSCRIPTION—8 issues—U.S. $19.95 USD; Canada $36.00 CDN (incl. GST and shipping); Foreign $25.95 USD
TWO-YEAR SUBSCRIPTION—16 issues—U.S. $35.95 USD; Canada $66.50 CDN (incl. GST and shipping); Foreign $47.95 USD

Printed and bound in USA by The Banta Company, Menasha, Wisconsin. Printed on Weyerhaeuser Husky.

The paper used in this publication meets the minimum requirements of
American National Standard for Information Sciences—Permanence of Paper for Printed Library Materials, ANSI Z39.48-1984.

Unsolicited manuscripts will not be returned without a self-addressed, stamped envelope.

ISBN 0-8249-1133-4   GST 131903775

Cover VALENTINES OF YESTERYEAR.
Al Riccio, Photographer.

Inside Front Cover THE SUITOR.
Postcard, c. 1900. Superstock.

Inside Back Cover COUPLE AT THE GARDEN GATE.
Postcard, c. 1900. Superstock.

Winter Valentine

Elisabeth Weaver Winstead

Snow feathers sail the dappled sky
   As glistening snowbirds flutter by.
The pine trees glow with silver frost
   Near lake with powdered sugar tossed.
Through filigrees of crystal lace,
   A thousand diamonds gleam in place.
Icicles sway in fringed design—
   That's winter's sparkling valentine.

Nature's Valentine

Eleanor Hammond

Frost-flowers on the window glass;
   Hopping chickadees that pass;
Bare old elms that bend and sway;
   Pussy willows, soft and gray;
Silver clouds across the sky;
   Lazy snowflakes flitting by;
Icicles like fringe in line—
   That is nature's valentine.

The Dream

Betty Harper Rohr

A sleigh behind a dappled horse
Glides over mounds of snow—
A scene relived in a pleasant dream
Of a world so long ago.

I see it all so vividly:
A land all crystal white
With lacy snowflakes drifting down
Unto a wondrous sight;

A blanket warm around me spread
To keep me from the cold
As sure hands firmly guide the horse
Back through a time of old.

When morning breaks and I awake
To face this world anew,
I wish that I might sleep again
And once more dream of you.

FUN IN THE SNOW
Original painting by Linda Nelson Stocks

Snowbirds

Mildred L. Jarrell

In spite of winter's skies of gray,
There's color round about today
With lovely snowbirds winging by
Mid bush and tree to catch the eye.

The chickadee with yellow vest
Stands out against the pine tree's crest,
And cardinals lend a jolly air
'Neath holly branch and berries there.

The blue jays gather round about
Whene'er I put the feeders out.
Their flutelike strain pervades the air
To telegraph the bill of fare.

A feeder for our feathered friends
Will bring a daily dividend
More pleasant than you've ever found
Whenever snowbirds gather round.

WINTER FAVORITES—
NORTHERN CARDINALS
Marc Hanson
Wild Wings, Inc.
Lake City, Minnesota

For You

Craig E. Sathoff

I'm looking for you, darling,
 Through meadows fresh with spring,
In autumn's gold-bespattered land,
 Through winter's covering.

I've never seen your gentle face;
 I've never heard your voice;
I've never shared my dreams with you;
 And yet, you are my choice.

I look for you in crowded rooms
 Or by the quiet stream.
I've seen you once or twice, my dear,
 Within a special dream.

I'm writing you these thoughts of love;
 And when at last you're mine,
I'll give to you this poem of love
 On our first Valentine's.

*"There are dreams
we must gather."*

—Jenny Walton

My Answer

Marion Doyle

Why do I love you?
    What a strange query!
Yet, I would say
    I'd never grow weary
Of telling to flower,
    Grass blade, and bird
The loveliest secret
    Ever they heard.

Why do I love you?
    I shouldn't wonder!
If laughter and tears,
    Soft music and thunder
Could blend all their voices
    To answer you true,
They'd say that I love you
    Because you are you.

Shared Silence

Mary E. Linton

Oh, I have shared your laughter,
    Your confidence, your tears.
I've felt the sudden closeness
    Of your voice upon my ears—
The one voice that enfolds me
    With gentle warmth set flowing—
But until I shared your silences,
    Mine was a lesser knowing.

YOUNG GIRL WRITING A LOVE LETTER
Johann Georg Meyer Von Bremen, 1813-1886
Josef Mensing Gallery, Hamm-Rhynern
Superstock

BITS & PIECES

My school-day valentines I've kept,
Some plain, some trimmed with lace;
And every one, within my heart,
Has its own special place.
Nadine Brothers Lybarger

My valentine I pray
That thou wilt be,
Not for a day,
But for eternity.
Charles Noel Douglas

Time flies, suns rise,
And shadows fall.
Let time go by.
Love is forever over all.
An Ancient Sundial

Memory is the power to gather roses in winter.
Author Unknown

I love thee to the level of every day's most quiet need, by sun and candlelight.
Elizabeth Barrett Browning

We cannot know what our dreams really mean until we mix them with those of someone we love.
Author Unknown

Sometimes love has been implanted by a single glance.
Burckhardt

Gail Roth

from
Renascence

Edna St. Vincent Millay

The world stands out on either side
No wider than the heart is wide;
Above the world is stretched the sky,
No higher than the soul is high.
The heart can push the sea and land
Farther away on either hand;
The soul can split the sky in two
And let the face of God shine through.

"After all, my erstwhile dear,
My no longer cherished,
Need we say it was not love
Just because it perished?"
—Edna St. Vincent Millay

LYNN CANAL
Tongass National Forest, Alaska
Jeff Gnass Photography

LEGENDARY AMERICANS

NANCY SKARMEAS

EDNA ST. VINCENT MILLAY

The poet Edna St. Vincent Millay was born in 1892 in Rockland, Maine, and grew up in nearby Camden, Maine, a harbor village nestled between Mt. Battie and the waters of Penobscot Bay. Known as Vincent at home, Millay was raised by her mother, a devoted woman whose work as a practical nurse often took her away from her daughters for days at a time. Millay and her sisters were frequently left to fend for themselves; but Cora Millay, divorced from an unreliable husband when Vincent was eight, did not expect her daughters to be dour children, burdened by the weight of family responsibilities. Cora Millay valued creativity, expression, and individuality over rules and strict discipline, and her daughters enjoyed a freedom that was unusual for young girls of that era.

They stayed up late reading, writing, performing plays, and practicing their music; they ate their meals whenever they pleased; and they devoted little energy to domestic order.

Vincent Millay blossomed in the rich and nurturing environment of her mother's home. Vincent was a bright and energetic young girl with striking red hair and green eyes. She began writing poetry at the age of five and saw her first work published in *St. Nicholas,* a magazine for children, when she was only fourteen.

Cora Millay instilled in her daughter a passion for independence and creativity that would guide her all the days of her life. Nonetheless, in 1912, Vincent Millay was twenty years old and still living with her family in Camden, waiting for the opportunity to make something of her life. In that year, on the urging of her mother, Millay sent her poem "Renascence" to the editors of the anthology *The Lyric Year* who were assembling an issue of the country's one hundred best new poems. Millay's symbolic poem told of a young woman's death and rebirth and drew its imagery from the striking scenery of coastal Maine. "Renascence" won a spot in the anthology and soon caught the eye of several influential people, among them Caroline Dow of the YMCA Women's Training School in New York City. Ms. Dow heard Millay read the poem at a talent show in Camden and was so impressed that she took the young poet under her wing. With Dow's guidance, Millay applied for and received a scholarship to Vassar College. A freshman at Vassar in 1913, Millay, so long anxious for a taste of the world beyond small-town Maine, sensed that her future was finally about to begin; she wrote to her mother, "I don't know where I am going, but I am on my way."

At Vassar, although she chafed at the strict discipline and regulations governing student behavior, Millay eventually flourished. She discovered a particular passion for the theater and even wrote and starred in her own production. Above all else, however, she continued to write poetry. By 1917, the year of her graduation from Vassar, Millay had her first published book of verse, *Renascence and Other Poems.*

From Vassar, Millay moved to Greenwich Village in New York City, where she became a popular part of a thriving artistic community. The independent, non-conformist Millay lived on her own in the city, unheard of for women of her day. She refused several early offers of marriage, preferring instead the freedom of her single life to the security of domesticity. She became a symbol of the American woman of the Roaring Twenties—confident, independent, and outspoken—and soon won acclaim as one of the nation's most promising young poets. The poetry of her New York days was brash and full of the bravado of youth, but it was also beautifully lyrical. In 1923, Edna St. Vincent Millay received the Pulitzer prize for *The Harp Weaver and Other Poems*, becoming the first woman to be awarded this distinguished honor.

Nineteen twenty-three was an important year in Millay's personal life as well. Although she had balked for years at the thought of marriage—she had no desire, she liked to say, to become as "domestic as a plate"—in that year the poet married Eugen Jan Boissevain, a Dutch businessman. With Boissevain, Millay enjoyed a rich, nurturing environment not unlike what she had known in her mother's home. Boissevain was devoted to Millay and gave up many of his own business interests to support and encourage her work as a writer. The couple left New York City for the more tranquil environment of homes in the Berkshire Mountains of Massachusetts and Ragged Island off the coast of Maine, but Millay continued to write and to publish poetry. Throughout the twenties and into the early thirties, Edna St. Vincent Millay remained one of the country's most beloved poets.

When World War II broke out in Europe, Millay was inspired by the plight of her husband's family who were trapped in German-occupied Holland. She turned her poetry from personal to political and published a book of verse, *Make Bright the Arrows*, aimed at convincing Americans to recognize the growing trouble worldwide. Critics and other poets alike called it propaganda and declared that Millay had sacrificed her artistic integrity to a political cause; but the poet was undaunted. When the United States entered the war, Millay continued her activism. She wrote a radio play, *The Murder of Lidice*, that had a pro-war, pro-Allies message; she volunteered with the Red Cross; and she joined the Writers' War Board.

The controversy over Millay's work during the war changed the way the public looked at her, and as new styles and poetic ideas came into vogue, her work fell out of favor. Millay's popularity never again reached the heights it had known in the Roaring Twenties. She died in 1950 at the age of fifty-eight, only one year after the loss of her beloved husband.

In her youth, Edna St. Vincent Millay spoke about independence and decried the conventional securities the world had to offer. She wrote the four-line poem "Second Fig" as a declaration of her life's philosophy:

> Safe upon the solid rock
> the ugly houses stand:
> Come and see my shining palace
> built upon the sand!

This and other poems of the poet's youth remain an inspiration to many, and the contribution she made to the emancipation of women in American society is acknowledged by all. Yet the true message of the poet's life as a whole is rather more complex. As a child and a young woman in a society that viewed women as dependent, Millay was blessed with her mother's unconditional love and support, which enabled her to leave Camden and seek out her place in the world. In the second half of her life, it was the same love and support provided by her husband that gave Millay the courage to pursue her art and to live her life by her own standards, even when that meant defying the opinions of her own literary community during World War II. Neither attachment rendered Millay dependent; both made her stronger. Edna St. Vincent Millay's life was built, after all, upon the "solid rock" that she so soundly dismissed in "Second Fig." With age, she must have come to understand that this truth made her independence more meaningful. In retrospect, it makes her life all the more inspirational.

Nancy Skarmeas is a book editor who enjoys knitting, running, and playing with her dalmations, Lucy and Riley, at her home in New Hampshire. Her Greek and Irish ancestry has fostered a lifelong interest in research and history.

The Long, White Seam

Jean Ingelow

As I came round the harbor buoy,
  The lights began to gleam.
No wave the landlocked water stirred;
  The crags were white as cream;
And I marked my love by candlelight
  Sewing her long, white seam.
    It's aye sewing ashore, my dear,
      Watch and steer at sea;
    It's reef and furl, and haul the line,
      Set sail and think of thee.

I climbed to reach her cottage door;
  Oh, sweetly my love sings!
Like a shaft of light her voice breaks forth;
  My soul to meet it springs
As the shining water leaped of old

When stirred by angel wings.
  Aye longing to list anew,
    Awake and in my dream,
  But never a song she sang like this,
    Sewing her long, white seam.

Fair fall the lights, the harbor lights,
  That brought me in to thee;
And peace drop down on that low roof
  For the sight that I did see
And for the voice, my dear, that rang so clear
  All for the love of me.
    For oh, for oh, with brows bent low
      By the candle's flickering gleam,
    Her wedding gown it was she wrought,
      Sewing the long, white seam.

907
GRAND TRUNK RAILWAY
BULLETIN DATE
TRAIN NO.
FROM
DUE
REMARKS
17 W
PORTLAND
GORHAM
16 E
MONTREAL
GORHAM
2:50 PM
DANVILLE
GORHAM
STANDARD TIME
RAILWAY EXPRESS AGENCY

Next~Door Valentine

D. A. Hoover

I heard the evening train go by,
Its lonesome whistle blowing.
I wished that I could be on board,
Ties cut, and I were going
To some adventure far away,
Perhaps to strange, new lands
To feed some inner restlessness
And occupy my hands.

That was before the girl next door
And before the honeyed vines
Wrapped us as one on her porch swing
Where moonbeams would dance and shine.
Her eyes could rival all the stars.
What was the need to roam?
For everything the heart could wish
Was right here close at home.

Aboard a Slower Train

June Masters Bacher

I always took the milk train
(Although uncertain why)—
Perhaps to watch each season
Swoop and dip the sky.
I always took the milk train;
And when the snow was deep,
There was refreshing silence
About a world asleep.
I always took the milk train
At evening and at dawn
To watch the warmth reflected
As lights came blinking on.

I always took the milk train
And watched Spring running in
With apricots in blossom
And pollen on her chin.
Nobody seemed to hurry;
And though we chugged along,
We caught up with the seasons
And joined them in their song.
We saw and heard things special;
I guess the reason's plain:
There's time for meditation
Aboard a slower train.

GORHAM STATION
New Hampshire
Gene Ahrens Photography

Acknowledging a Gift of Roses

Alice J. Christianson

The doorbell rings,
And suddenly my life seems very bright
As in my arms
I gently bear the slender box so white
Into the quiet of my room
And carefully untie
The pretty bow then lift the lid,
Excitement running high.

There, in a bed
Of softest green, twelve scarlet roses rest,
Each perfect bloom
A message saying, "Dear, I love you best."
A poet said, "Love is a rose."
I'm sure that this is true,
Especially when the roses
Are sent to me by you.

How carefully
I place each flower against the feathery fern,
One here, one there,
One high, one low, so that each bloom will turn
Its pretty petal face to me
As patiently I wait
To hear your footsteps on the walk,
The latch-click of the gate.

But now each rose
Has opened wide, its tender heart revealing;
And sweet perfume,
Unchanged by time, across the room is stealing.
The candle flame,
An amber glow, your hand in mine discloses;
And faintly, through the shadows, comes
A rustling of roses.

Bouquet

Roy A. A. Blokker

I wish that they could all be roses
and that we were eating caviar
and that I could take you
casually
to Paris for dinner
and some shopping at Montmartre.
But they're not.
Someday, in time.
Always, always in time.
After ten years I guess daisies
and fish sticks
can be special
if you know where they come from
and dream with me
of where we might yet go.

Editor's Note: Readers are invited to submit unpublished, original poetry for possible publication in future issues of Ideals. *Please send typed copies only; manuscripts will not be returned. Writers receive $10 for each published submission. Send material to Readers' Reflections, Ideals Publications Inc., 535 Metroplex Drive, Suite 250, Nashville, Tennessee 37211.*

WHAT YOU ARE TO ME

I am a rose, you are my thorns,
Clutching to me, protecting me.
I am the sun, you are my rays,
Helping me to shine and to be all that I can.

I am a lake, you are my water,
Filling me with ideas, dreams,
    and hopes for the future.

I am a tree, you are my leaves,
Sharing who and what I am
    and becoming an important part of my life.

I am a heart, you are my beat,
Beating rhythmically to my happiness,
    my fear, my sadness, my excitement.

I am me and you are with me,
To share all that I am—
To share life, love, and happiness, always.

    Safronia Collins
    Newton, West Virginia

NOSTALGIA

How can it be?
Is Al really sixty-three?
Long ago when we were teens,
He was the object of my dreams.

He weighed one hundred pounds, soaking wet;
His brown eyes I would not forget.
He was my Tyrone Power, my Errol Flynn;
But, as I recall, he had no chin.

To mature and marry, we made plans.
Dad would laugh; he called it "glands."
By now Al has migraines and arthritis,
Going through his mid-life crisis.

To be heard, you'd have to shout;
He'd have pills to ease his gout.
To think of Al as old Granddad
Makes me nervous, even sad.

To see him now, would my heart flutter,
My knees turn to jelly, my soul to butter?
Somehow old Al evokes not a blush.
I think I've lost my teen-age crush.

    Louise C. Klein
    Bloomfield Hills, Michigan

MY VALUABLES

To you, it's just a shoebox full of things that are old.
To me, it's a treasure chest lined with silver and gold.

Some faded snapshots that were favorites of mine;
Some red velvet ribbon, and a special valentine;

A large yellowed envelope with letters inside
From a very dear friend who has long since died;

Half a theater ticket dated nineteen-fifty-four;
A key that used to open our first front door;

A tiny pearl necklace from the five-and-dime;
Some newspaper clippings of a happier time;

My graduation ring and the tassel from my cap;
A program with my favorite teacher's autograph;

A priceless curly lock of my little boy's hair,
Retrieved as it fell from the local barber's chair;

A shiny gold pendant that always makes me sad,
The last gift of love from my mom and dad.

Yes, to you, it looks like trash that somebody's left.
But to me, it's a place where memories are kept.

Mary Horner
Paducah, Kentucky

ODE TO THE GOLDEN YEARS

The beauty of our youth has long since gone
Though our love remains forever strong.
We've had our trials down through the years.
We've had our fun and shed our tears.
We may have slowed a step or two,
But just give up we'll never do.
With gnarled and twisted fingers clasped,
We'll savor our friendship to the last.

Eugene Mendini
Waukesha, Wisconsin

A DOZEN ROSES

I got a dozen roses
    from a friend the other day;
But I only have one left,
    for I gave them all away.

I gave one to my mother,
    who to me is very dear,
In hopes that it will bring to her
    a little floral cheer.

I took one to a friend
    who's not feeling very well;
The flower or the visit—
    which helped more I could not tell.

One went to a friend
    I haven't known for very long.
She struggles, so in some small way
    I hope this helps her carry on.

The rest went to the ones
    who've helped me in so many ways;
They have been a cheerful presence
    on my very dreary days.

The roses were so pretty
    I just could not keep them all,
Except one single bud standing
    beautiful and tall.

My friend gave me the flowers
    to help brighten up my day,
But the biggest joy I received
    was in giving them away.

Verlynn Marie Rader
Everett, Washington

CORNER

ANTIQUE CAMERAS by Michelle Prater Burke

In my mother's living room, an ornate, antique table stands covered with dozens of old photographs. Since I was a young girl, I have been fascinated by the sepia-colored images staring from out of the frames. Particularly striking is the picture of a stylishly dressed lady with her hair pulled back in a twist. My mother explains that this photograph of my grandmother was taken shortly after her engagement to my grandfather in 1932.

Having grown up visiting my grandmother's house frequently, I know where I get my passion for photography. My grandmother has always snapped photographs at every occasion. But as a child, her photographs did not interest me as much as her collection of old cameras in the attic. I loved to explore that dusty attic, and those old cameras always captivated my interest. I was especially intrigued with one made of black enamel with collapsing bellows, which I later learned was a 1936 Kodak Bantam Special. To this day, it is no surprise to me that collectors search out these antique cameras and remain fascinated with their ability to capture a visual record of our lives.

In 1839, history was made as the first photographic cameras were sold. This accomplishment was the result of years of experiments by individuals such as French inventor Joseph Nicéphore Niepce, who produced what is now the oldest surviving photograph around 1827; and artist Louis Jacques Mandé Daguerre, who created an early photographic process called daguerreotype and was dubbed the father of photography.

Advances in camera technology came quickly. The plain boxes and simple lenses of the 1830s soon evolved into complicated folding cameras of mahogany and teak. By the 1850s, the camera sat on a tripod; and photographers had to cover their heads with a dark cloth to block the light from the sun in order to view the image on the screen.

By the Civil War, cameras allowed photographers such as Mathew Brady to chronicle the events of war extensively for the first time. But the wet-plate cameras of the time were so complicated and cumbersome that they were often used by professionals only. Gelatin dry-plate cameras replaced wet-plate cameras by 1878.

In 1888, entrepreneur George Eastman introduced a box camera called the Kodak that was aimed at the amateur market. The original Kodak was a box camera that came with a 100-image roll of paper film—all for a cost of $25 (about $350 at today's prices). After shooting the film, the consumer sent the entire camera back to the manufacturer where the film was printed and the camera reloaded and returned. Thus, the snapshot was born; and by the turn of the century, cameras were available to practically any eager shutterbug.

Cameras continued to develop throughout the years as interest and innovations continued. Panoramic cameras, which were introduced to capture landscapes and groups of people, became widely available in 1896. By early 1913, the first 35-millimeter camera appeared on the market, and a nifty flash device was out by the 1920s. The modern camera was becoming a reality.

After so many years of development, a multitude of camera styles are available to collectors; and an interested collector should always start with some research to determine where his or her interests lie. Some collectors seek out cameras from a specific historical era, such as the highly sought after German pre-World War II cameras by makers such as Leica. Or they may favor models by a specific manufacturer; for example, Deardorff's classic styles and Kodak's numerous innovations often draw interest from collectors. A collection may also feature cameras that chronicle new developments in technology, such as the Super Kodak Six-20 of 1938, which introduced automatic exposure.

Although film for old or rare models is often hard to come by, many antique models are still fully functional for those who want to use even their oldest camera. Some collectors ignore mechanics and

DEARDORFF CAMERA. Superstock.

instead choose pieces based on visual appeal or period style, such as the disguised cameras that were immensely popular in the 1880s or the stylish art deco models from the 1930s.

Perhaps the strongest reason collectors are drawn to particular cameras is because of sentiment and memory. You might select a palm-sized Kodak Brownie camera, first introduced in 1900, as a remembrance of your first camera as a child. Or maybe a classic model with bellows will bring back memories of cherished photos of family vacations.

Depending on your interests, investment costs vary greatly. The quaint Kodak Brownies can be found for only a few dollars, but pre-World War II models can be priced into the thousands. While discerning value is often difficult for both seasoned collectors and novices, value often depends on a camera's condition or its rarity. Smooth operation is always a plus with cameras that still work, and any bellows should be free of pinholes.

Camera connoisseurs discover their finds in a variety of places. Some specialty stores can offer savvy advice along with a variety of intriguing models. Antique cameras often hide upon the cluttered tables of flea markets, or a determined collector may spot advertisements for old cameras in the back of photography magazines.

Whether your collection centers around several inexpensive, memorable styles or a few choice pieces from the early days of the camera, you can relish the idea that a camera you find may have once focused on an Allied soldier or a 1960s piano recital. Or perhaps the favorite camera in your collection once snapped the picture of a stylish young woman in the 1930s who would one day pass her love for cameras on to her ever-grateful granddaughter.

On weekend excursions throughout the South, Michelle Prater Burke sharpens her eagle eye while searching for hidden treasures. Her best advice to aspiring collectors is that the price is always negotiable!

A Song

Hildegarde Hawthorne

Sing me a sweet, low song of night
Before the moon is risen,
A song that tells of the stars' delight
Escaped from the day's bright prison,

A song that croons with the cricket's voice,
    That sleeps with the shadowed trees,
A song that shall bid my heart rejoice
    At its tender mysteries!

And then when the song is ended, Love,
    Bend down your head unto me,
Whisper the word that was born above
    Ere the moon had swayed the sea,

Ere the oldest star began to shine,
    Or the farthest sun to burn—
The oldest of words, O heart of mine,
    Yet newest, and sweet to learn.

HANDMADE HEIRLOOM

BROKEN CHINA MOSAIC FRAME. Frame crafted by Michelle Prater Burke. Jerry Koser Photography.

BROKEN CHINA MOSAIC FRAME

Mary Skarmeas

Not long ago, my daughter received a special gift from her mother-in-law, a beautiful china teacup and saucer—delicate white china with a thin band of gold trim and a green tartan pattern. The cup and saucer belonged to my son-in-law's grandmother in Nova Scotia; it was a gift that symbolized love and family connection, a true heirloom. Not long after, the cup fell from a dining room shelf and shattered beyond repair. My daughter, heartbroken over the loss, gathered the pieces and stored them in a drawer, so reluctant was she to discard them. It was pure serendipity that I happened to call a few days later—unaware of the broken teacup—and mention that I recently had heard of using broken china to create a decorative mosaic picture frame. The idea gave my daughter hope for salvaging her antique china cup and the opportunity to turn a misfortune into a delightful mosaic craft that in itself becomes an heirloom to pass on.

Its vibrant colors and eye-catching patterns have made mosaics both a popular art medium and a creative craft idea. Mosaic art combines small pieces of stone, tile, glass, or other material on a surface to create one unified design. This unique art form has quite a long history. Archaeologists have discovered mosaics from the ancient civilizations that once lived in the valleys of the Euphrates and Tigris rivers. Dating back to around 3000 B.C., these ancient mosaics adorned items ranging from architectural structures to beautiful jewelry.

Through the years, the Egyptians, Greeks, and Romans experimented with and perfected many mosaic styles and techniques. Years of practice and a mastery of the craft led to the creation of the breathtaking, lifelike mosaic designs that adorn so many of the old-world churches and cathedrals in Europe.

For years, mosaics remained an art form for only professional artists, who strictly guarded their carefully developed techniques. After World War II, however, Americans began to vacation in Italy, where they discovered the spectacular mosaics of the European churches. The tourists brought a love for mosaics home with them, and it was this interest that led to the popular craft of today.

One of the most appealing characteristics of mosaics is that it offers such a wide variety of possible materials, designs, and projects. The earliest mosaics used fragments of natural materials such as marble and precious stones placed into a base made of wood or bone. Later, pieces of glass and ceramics became the materials of choice. The mosaic crafts of today feature everything from broken china and colorful pottery to tinted glass and patterned tiles. The beautiful patterns and cherished appeal of china in particular make it an excellent choice, especially when creating a mosaic craft of heirloom status.

After gathering all the broken cups and saucers you've saved through the years, deciding what mosaic project to take on may be difficult, for your choices are endless. Mosaics can decorate all kinds of items, both indoors and out, and projects include everything from colorful table tops to garden stepping stones. One charming way to reuse your cherished china pieces and display them in your home is to design a mosaic frame.

Any wide, flat frame will make a suitable surface for the small pieces of china that you will use. The wider the surface area, the greater the options and also the greater the amount of china needed. You may wish to glue thin wood molding around the perimeter of the frame in order to form a raised, finished edge that will contain the grout and eliminate any sharp, exposed edges. You can paint the trim to complement your china pattern.

Obviously, a dropped teacup or chipped plate will not be broken to the right size for a frame—you will need to do some fine breaking of your own. Wear safety glasses and sturdy gloves and work on a large, flat surface. Use either tile nippers or a hammer—wielded gently and carefully—to break the china, and be extremely careful when handling the sharp, broken pieces. Flat pieces of china are easier to work with and produce a smoother finished frame.

When the pieces are ready, try arranging them on a cardboard template drawn to the size of the frame. Rearrange the pieces until you decide on a pleasing design for the entire template. The pieces need not meet up edge to edge; grout will fill in any gaps and create a smooth surface.

For the finishing step, you will need unsanded, all-purpose grout, which may be colored. Spread the grout onto the frame one small section at a time. Immediately transfer a section of china pieces to the grouted areas, working quickly to recreate the pattern you designed on your template. Press each piece firmly into the grout and wipe off any excess grout with a slightly damp towel. Continue applying grout and china to the frame one small area at a time until all pieces are in place and no excess grout remains. Allow the completed frame to dry thoroughly before adding your favorite photograph.

Perhaps one of the allures of mosaics is its ability to bring seemingly mismatched elements together in harmony. Think of my daughter's broken china cup, once passed down from mother to daughter to daughter-in-law. She could leave those pieces of china in that drawer and always regret the loss of such a treasured gift; or with a little time and ingenuity, she could transform an accident into a new family keepsake. My daughter is expecting her first child in a few months, and there is perhaps no better gift for her mother-in-law than a picture of the new baby framed by bits of heirloom china—the perfect mosaic of a unique family history.

Mary Skarmeas lives in Danvers, Massachusetts, and is studying for her bachelor's degree in English at Suffolk University. Mother of four and grandmother of one, Mary loves all crafts, especially knitting.

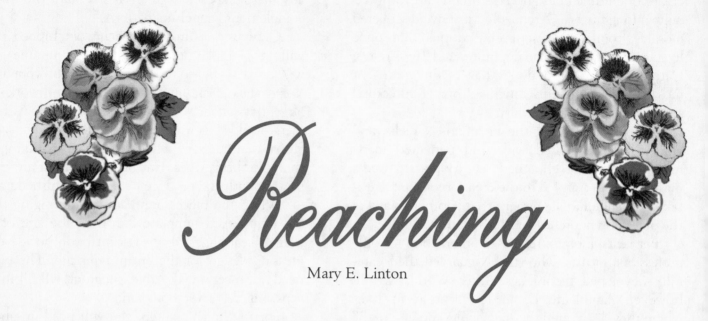

Reaching

Mary E. Linton

Because you love me I would make
My whole life nobler for your sake.
Because you trust me I would be
All things that you believe of me.

You think me strong, you little know;
But since you do, I strive, I grow.
You help me build a world today
Of age-enduring brick from clay.

Because you have believed in me
I shall believe in life, and see,
Through your firm faith, a higher view,
Design and purpose carried through.

Because you love me I would rise
To fit the picture in your eyes,
To reach, attain, at last set free
My full potentiality.

A SLICE OF LIFE

Edgar A. Guest

To a Little Girl

Little girl, just half past three,
    Take this little rhyme from me:
All the joy that gold can bring,
    All the songs the birds can sing,
All this world can hold to give
    Grown-up men the while they live
Hath not half the charm of you
    And the lovely things you do.

Little girl, just half past three,
    When God sent you down to me,
Oft I wonder, did He know
    Fortune's power would dwindle so?
Did He know that I should find
    Such a curious change of mind
And should someday come to see
    Just how trivial pomp can be?

Little girl, just half past three,
    Lost are dreams that used to be.
Now the things I thought worthwhile
    Could not buy your lovely smile,
And I would not give you up
    For the golden plate and cup
And the crown a king may boast.
    In my life you're uppermost.

Little girl, just half past three,
    This is what you mean to me,
More than all that money buys,
    More than any selfish prize,
More than fortune, more than fame;
    And I learned this when you came.
Other fathers know it, too.
    Nothing matters more than you.

Edgar A. Guest began his illustrious career in 1895 at the age of fourteen when his work first appeared in the Detroit Free Press. *His column was syndicated in over 300 newspapers, and he became known as "The Poet of the People."*

Valentine Shopper

Mary Louise Sanker

What can I give you that will not cost much?
The counters are covered with clothing and such.
Some things are too costly, some trifles, it seems.
What can I give you? I'll give you my dreams.

What can I find where red, satin hearts bloom?
In a froth of white lace and a hint of perfume,
Here is Cupid's own courier, a swift-winging dove.
But I'll buy none of these—I will give you my love.

So I search through the mart, at this counter and that,
Swinging lightly my purse, which is thriftlessly flat.
Out of all of these wares I will purchase no part.
What, then, can I offer? I'll give you my heart.

A Special Valentine

William Arnette Wofford

I could not find a valentine
Upon the counter that would do,
Or any, Mother, that expressed
The special love I have for you.

No rhyme told just how kind you are;
Not one described the magic way
Your lovely, gentle smile can make
Bleak winter skies as fair as May.

Oh, who could know as well as I
That you're the one to me most dear
And that I'll love you more and more
With every passing month and year?

So on this day of bright red hearts,
I'm glad to tell the joy that's mine
And send you, Mother, this rhymed verse,
Which is your special valentine.

For Mother

Marna G. Simons

Busy little fingers
Concentrate so hard
On cutting stiff red paper
In heart shapes for her card.
He hands his card to Mother—
Its sticky paste not dry—
And understands the meaning
Of the tear that's in her eye.

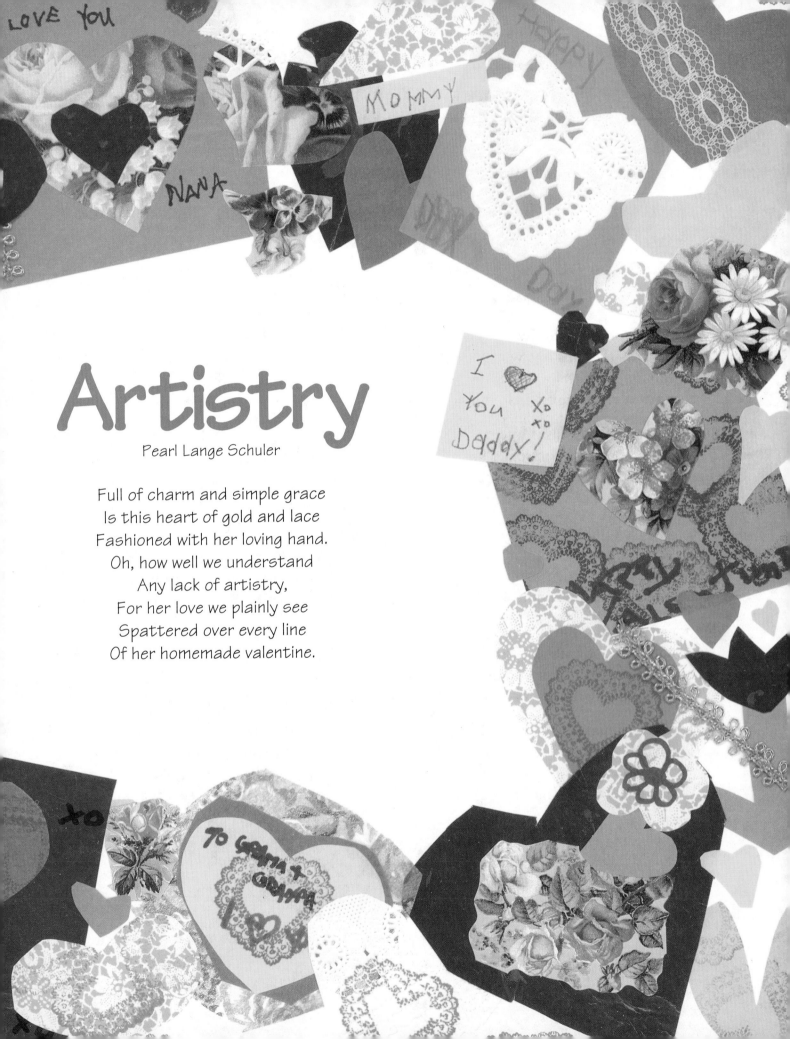

Artistry

Pearl Lange Schuler

Full of charm and simple grace
Is this heart of gold and lace
Fashioned with her loving hand.
Oh, how well we understand
Any lack of artistry,
For her love we plainly see
Spattered over every line
Of her homemade valentine.

THE SMACK IN SCHOOL

William Pitt Palmer

A district school, not far away,
   Mid Berkshire hills one winter's day
Was humming with its wonted noise
   Of threescore mingled girls and boys,

Some few upon their tasks intent,
   But more on furtive mischief bent.
The while the master's downward look
   Was fastened on a copybook;

When suddenly, behind his back,
   Rose sharp and clear a rousing smack,
As 'twere a battery of bliss
   Let off in one tremendous kiss!

"What's that?" the startled master cried.
   "That, Thir," a little imp replied,
"Wath William Willith, if you pleathe—
   I thaw him kith Thuthannah Peathe!"

With frown to make a statue thrill,
   The master thundered, "Hither, Will!"
Like wretch o'ertaken in his track
   With stolen chattels on his back,

Will hung his head in fear and shame;
   And to the awful presence came
A great, green, bashful simpleton,
   The butt of all good-natured fun.

With smile suppressed and birch upraised,
   The threatener faltered, "I'm amazed
That you, my biggest pupil, should
   Be guilty of an act so rude!

Before the whole set school to boot—
   What evil genius put you to't?"
"'Twas she herself, sir," sobbed the lad,
   "I did not mean to be so bad;

But when Susannah shook her curls
   And whispered I was 'fraid of girls
And dursn't kiss a baby's doll,
   I couldn't stand it, sir, at all,

But up and kissed her on the spot!
   I know, boohoo, I ought to not;
But somehow, from her looks, boohoo,
   I thought she kind of wished me to!"

John Slobodnik

THE ANTIPODES
E. P.

Here all the world is wintertime,
　And gusty breezes blow
On violets that sleep beneath
　A counterpane of snow.

The sparrows huddle in the rain
　Or hardly try to sing,
But go to bed at five instead
　To dream about the spring.

And yet, in the Antipodes—
　A word I learned last week
With several other pleasant terms
　(They tell me that it's Greek)—

In Sydney and Van Diemen's Land,
　December days are bright;
And while we mourn a winter day,
　They sing a summer night.

'Tis winter here, 'tis summer there;
　Likewise in every town
They justify the weather chart
　By walking upside-down.

Now, I should like, when summer's gone
　And winter brings the rain,
To turn the world the wrong way round
　And find the spring again!

The unique perspective of Russ Flint's artistic style has made him a favorite of Ideals *readers for many years. A resident of California and father of four, Russ Flint has illustrated a children's Bible and many other books.*

The Valentine Crush

Talbert A. Pond

Some of the simplest things can trigger special memories hidden in the recesses of our minds. It can be a song, a favorite dessert, or a flower in a field. For me it was a plain, white envelope. My daughter was holding it in her hand while reading the valentine that she was selecting for someone special.

"Dad, what do you think of this one?" she asked.

"I like the envelope," I replied.

She was giving me that look which said that her father finally went off the deep end. She didn't realize that the envelope was taking me back to another Valentine's Day thirty years ago. I was recalling a one-room schoolhouse; another plain, white envelope; a cute, dark-haired girl with pigtails; and a boy of twelve who was first noticing girls.

In those days, most twelve-year-old boys referred to girls as "those girls," and when you said it, you were required to have a sound of disgust in your voice. Other than your mother, the only two females you could like (if you wanted to still be accepted by your best buddies) were Dale Evans and Lassie. Back then we didn't know Hollywood had placed a male dog in Lassie's role.

I swore I didn't like girls, but I was getting quite interested in the dark-haired girl with pigtails who sat opposite from me in class. On the upcoming Valentine's Day, I was going to make my big move—maybe.

February fourteenth was always a red-letter day at school. Everyone enjoyed cake and cookies after the cards were passed out at the day's end. A large cardboard box with a slot in the top was always decorated by the younger students. It contained all the valentines, and the teacher allowed none of us near it after we deposited our cards. When the time came to pass out the valentines, the teacher gave only the receiver's name, not the giver's, so no one teased anyone else. One other rule was that you had to give one card to each student, so no one would be left out.

Now this rule meant that you had to give even your worst enemy a card, but it didn't stop you from choosing the most insulting card for him. It didn't keep you from putting a nickname he hated on it, and it didn't rule out crumbling up the card a little and spilling jam on it for good measure.

Serious thought went into choosing each individual card. Mother would buy us a book of valentines that had five sheets plus front and back covers. Each of the sheets contained five cards. The book's front cover folded up into the fancy valentine, while the back cover folded into an envelope for the front valentine. The cost for the whole book was a mere ninety-eight cents.

When selecting which card to give, there were many unwritten rules to follow. The funniest cards went to your buddies, the small, cute cards went to the younger students, and you never sent a card with the word *love* on it to a girl. The large card was always the hardest decision; some boys saved it for their mother. In the past, I always gave it to the teacher, but this year was different. I made up my mind; I put the name of the dark-haired girl with pigtails on the big, fancy valentine.

The big day arrived; and, luckily, I got my cards in the decorated box without anyone seeing them. When the cards disappeared into the box, my first reaction was "Wow, I did it!" Soon, I started to sweat. Did I do the right thing? Would she make fun of my card? Would she show it to the other girls, especially "Big Mouth" and "Giggles"? I was panicking so much that I was almost ready to ram my hand into the large box, retrieve my card, and tear it up. But then the dark-haired girl walked in. She looked my way and smiled. Suddenly, I was calm—well, calmer.

I noticed everything about her, but what really caught my eye were her cards as she dropped them into the box. They were store-bought cards with white envelopes, not cut-outs like the rest of us. She had about twenty small ones and one large one. My imagination started to work overtime. Was that big white envelope for me? I let my dreams run wild for a while; but, finally, I surmised that the big envelope was probably for the teacher.

The morning and afternoon seemed to go by so slowly, but finally it came—the time to pass out cards. My palms began to sweat. The teacher shook the large box and started calling out names and handing out cards. Halfway into the presentation of valentines, I suddenly noticed my card in the teacher's hand and heard her call the dark-haired girl's name. I could feel my body starting to get sweaty again, but I held it in check until my curiosity finally got the best of me. Dropping my pencil and bending to pick it up, I glanced in her direction. "Big Mouth" was busting with curiosity as she waited for her friend to open that big valentine, but she didn't open it like the others. She slipped it in her bookbag, slung the bag into her lap to protect it, and then turned in my direction. She had the cutest smile on her face. I just knew I had had a hundred-pound weight lifted off my shoulders, and I was now in dreamland.

Suddenly, I realized someone was poking me in the arm. It was my buddy John. He was pointing to the teacher. "She called your name three times already. Wake up!"

Wake up I did. Not because of the look on my teacher's face, which she always got when I daydreamed in her class, but from what she held in her hand. She was holding a large, white, store-bought envelope; and she was calling my name.

I almost knocked over the desk getting out of it, but I caught myself in time and slowed down my emotions so that nobody really noticed that I was on fire inside. Finally, I had the envelope securely in my grasp and was back in my seat. I slowly looked down at the writing on the outside, and a funny sensation ran through me that I had never felt before. It was her handwriting. I glanced in her direction and smiled and got a smile back. John was poking me to open the envelope. I didn't. I waited until all the cards were passed out. I waited until everyone went up front for cookies and cake. I waited until everyone's back was to me. Then, I made for the door. It must have been love—I had never passed up cookies and cake before.

When I was about a mile away from school, in my favorite spot on my favorite rock, I slowly opened the envelope. It was a valentine all right, but inside she had mercilessly penned, "I gave this to you to make John jealous. Do you think he likes me?" My heart sank. Do I think he likes her? No! He doesn't even like Dale Evans! I was dumb struck. She was supposed to like me! I couldn't believe my plan had backfired.

I could feel my ears turning beet red from jealousy. I debated for quite a while whether or not even to show the card to John, but I finally did. Hiding my overwhelming curiosity, I asked him, "Do you think she wants you to kiss her?" John said he'd rather kiss a horse. I agreed. With a sigh of relief, I inwardly thanked him for being such a good friend.

So are the ways of grade-school romances and the crushes of twelve-year-old boys. Even though I managed to grow up and get over my valentine crush, I have always valued that first, hard-earned lesson in love. And I'll always have a soft spot in my heart for dark hair and pigtails.

My First Valentine

Esther Cushman Randall

There are cards of scenic beauty;
    Cards of sacred prose and rhyme;
Prints and etchings of the Old Masters
    That will never fade with time;
Cards that shine like silvered moonbeams,
    Filigreed, embossed, and fine;
But there'll never be one nicer
    Than my first red valentine.

It was in a country schoolhouse
    When I, a lassie just past nine,
Had the joyous, thrilling pleasure
    Of my first red valentine.
Just a penny, not so fancy,
    But that captivating line—
"I love you"—leaves a magic
    From my first red valentine.

My Favorite Valentine Memory

Personal Stories of Treasured Memories from the Ideals Family of Readers

A Gift from the Heart

I have always considered myself to be a romantic at heart. Ever since I was a young girl, I have been unable to resist a good love story; and Valentine's Day has always been my most revered holiday. Each year I would lavish my loved ones with ornate cards, chocolate hearts, and an abundance of roses, and I would always expect the same in return. After all, I was a true romantic.

So when my fiancé and I were planning our wedding, I had my heart set on only one date: February 14. Our Valentine's Day wedding the following year seemed to be the ultimate romantic gesture. I could think of no better way to start many years of wedded bliss, and I cherished the thought that we could spend that special day each year celebrating our anniversary.

But as our one-year anniversary approached, my heart just wasn't in it. I was teaching fifth grade at a local school and my husband was struggling through graduate classes, so there was no money for the romantic celebration that I had always planned. I was heartbroken.

The night of our anniversary, I hid my disappointment as my husband walked in without any bouquets or elegantly wrapped gifts. He quietly handed me a small, modest card, and my eyes filled with tears as I read the simple words: "You are every flower and every gift that I could ever wish for. There is no greater valentine than knowing you love me."

As February nears each year, I still spend weeks anticipating this special holiday. Although years have passed and my Valentine's Days are once again filled with chocolates and the sweet scent of roses, it is that first Valentine's as a newlywed that I remember most tenderly. A few heartfelt words taught me that true romance can only be felt, not given. Love in itself is a very valuable gift, and perhaps the sweetest gift of all.

Anna Sarkissi
Denver, Colorado

The Snowflake

I remember a very special Valentine's Day almost twenty years ago when my oldest child, Michael, was in second grade. I had always made a big deal of Valentine's Day at home with lots of special treats and presents. That year I made some extra goodies and took them in to share with Michael's entire class. When I arrived, the class was busily crafting valentines. I asked the teacher, Mrs. Colvin, if I could help, and she gladly led me to a small boy named John who was sitting

off to the side. Mrs. Colvin whispered to me that he was a bit slower than the other children and needed more attention. John was clearly having difficulty manipulating his scissors, but he looked up at me with a bright, happy smile as I joined him. His smile faded, though, as he handed his strangled paper over to me and asked for help. I smiled at him and said a quick prayer as I carefully took his "valentine." After turning the paper around a few times, I decided it might be safest to turn it into a snowflake, which would hopefully disguise any cuts gone awry. Meanwhile, Michael had finished his valentine and had joined John and me. After a few daring snips of the scissors, I carefully unfolded John's creation. His face lit up the classroom as the snowflake emerged. As I watched Michael quietly help John glue the snowflake onto a piece of colored paper, I realized that there are more ways to bring happiness to others on Valentine's Day than with sweets and presents. John and I had shared a special moment of joy.

Lacy C. Jernigan
Des Moines, Iowa

A Garden of Love

Growing up, my sister and I often accompanied my grandparents to visit friends at Glen Haven Rest Home. I was always impressed with the infectiousness of Grandma's good cheer. We'd plan to visit a few specific people, but generally would end up meeting and greeting almost everyone there. It was always an uplifting experience; making friends and hearing tales of times long gone made the day just a little bit brighter for everyone.

On one particular visit, my sister and I helped Grandma plant tulip bulbs and crocuses in a small flower bed outside the sitting room. Each visit after that we'd spend a few minutes weeding and tending to our little garden gift. Grandma's entertaining stories and the smiles of residents made the time spent working in the soil fly by.

Years later, after Grandma passed away, I was home visiting my family on Valentine's Day and thought I'd accompany my grandfather on a visit to Glen Haven. I was feeling melancholy as I remembered that the last time I was there, Grandma had been there too. The smiles of friends at Glen Haven cheered me a bit, but it wasn't until I looked out the window that I really perked up. There, under the light layer of snow that had fallen that morning, I saw the outline of our little garden. Walking outside to take a closer look, I noticed the crocuses popping their little purple blooms up through the snow, straining for the sun to help them grow stronger. I smiled through tears of happiness as I remembered that day shared with my sister and Grandma as we started the little garden that had flourished through the years. I realized that just as that flower bed was still strong as a result of my grandmother's nurturing hands, I too had become a stronger person because of her love.

Long ago, Grandma told me, "Miracles happen every day; we've just become so busy that we often fail to notice them." On that special Valentine's Day, I realized just how true those words really are.

Marisa Lennox
Boston, Massachusetts

Souvenirs

I watched him tugging at the heavy doors in the store's entrance. Soon he returned to the car with a smile belonging exclusively to five-year-olds—or maybe angels.

"Mom, here's your valentine," he said.

From out of the sack tumbled a pair of scarlet, heart-shaped, plastic earscrews marked twenty-five cents.

Forty years have gone by. I still proudly wear these souvenirs of a child's love on each Valentine's Day; to me they are as precious as the rarest diamonds!

Faye Field
Longview, Texas

Pup in the Snowstorm

Frances Frost

My lop-eared pup looked up at me
   With dark, accusing eyes
And plainly asked, "What seems to be
   The matter with the skies?"
He was so young; he'd never seen
   The lovely snow before.
He sat down on his wagging tail
   Before our drifted door
And rose as promptly, turned round
   To stare at where he'd sat,
Amazed that happy earth could be
   As sudden-cold as that!

I laughed, but with a puzzled look
   He pawed and reared into
A drift and scrambled madly there,
   Trying to get through.
With silver on his nose and brows
   And silver on his coat,
He gazed askance at any skies
   Gone suddenly afloat.
Out of the drift he trotted then
   And snapped up snowflakes, bound
And determined to catch all the sky
   Before it touched the ground.

SAMOYED PUPPIES
Superstock

THROUGH MY WINDOW

Pamela Kennedy

Art by Russ Flint

VALENTINES FOREVER

They met when they were only five and six years old, a little girl and boy whose parents owned adjacent summer homes on a saltwater beach in Seattle. At first, they spent their time together just digging for clams, searching for tiny crabs under barnacle-encrusted rocks, and splashing in the sun-warmed water. Years passed, and as they grew, they whiled away their summer days paddling a polished, wooden canoe to secret coves and stretches of beach where alder trees grew thick to the water's edge. They shared their dreams and teen-aged heartaches with one another in the secure intimacy that only best friends know. And in their adolescent assurance, he carved their names inside a heart on an alder tree, and they promised to be valentines forever.

During school terms, she commuted to an exclusive private girl's academy to learn Latin, algebra, and etiquette. He attended the local public high school, worked part time on the Seattle shipping docks, and played football. For nine months of the year, they lived in different worlds, but summer brought them close again to fill their days with sun-drenched hours of conversation. There were other friends, romances, and adolescent dramas played out on their separate stages, but always they returned to the deeply rooted friendship planted in their summers at the beach.

After high school graduation, she headed east with her family to tour the United States while he began premed studies at the University of Washington. Upon her return some months later, she moved onto the same campus to study drama and literature. Now and then their paths crossed as they walked to class or met in the Student Union Building, and their easy friendship led to conversations reminiscent of the summer days of childhood.

In the winter of 1942, after the bombs of Pearl Harbor and Roosevelt's call to arms, young men left their college campuses, eager to defend their country and fight in the Pacific. And so she watched him leave for flight training with a smile on her face but an aching heart. She promised to write and pray for his safety, all the while wondering if their paths would ever cross again.

From Corpus Christi, Texas, came letters describing the thrill of flight training and the challenges and excitement of being a naval officer. She smiled, remembering the young boy who taught her to bait a hook and who fended off imaginary sea monsters with a canoe paddle. Soon his enemies would be all too real. She kept her fears inside, prayed harder, and sent letters filled with happy reminiscences of a time when summers were simply to be enjoyed.

His parents called one day to say they were off to Texas to visit him and asked if she would like to ride along. They thought they'd surprise him and tour a bit of the country in the process. On a lark, she decided to go.

It wasn't the young boy she remembered who met them at the Naval Air Station, nor the glib fraternity man from campus. It was someone she knew as well as herself, yet someone who was now also a stranger. He looked at her with different eyes as well. The tomboy he had chased through alder trees and fern thickets was a lovely young woman. Their friendship was at once old and new. Touched with an awakening love, they saw in one another not only their shared past but also the exciting promise of their future as well. Asked later how it had happened, neither had an explanation; it was just as right and natural as walking, one step necessarily following the other.

Within three months his leave was arranged and a wedding planned. They walked down the aisle as husband and wife, best friends and confidantes. They were not so much beginning their lives together as they were continuing them, side by side.

In time, the war ended, homes were bought and sold, careers were established, two sons were born and grew up. The couple weathered illnesses and difficult times in business, buried their parents, and celebrated the birth of grandchildren. They experienced life together in its many stages. And through it all they were friends—friends who fought and made up, who suffered and endured, who laughed and cried together.

Now they face another milestone—their golden wedding anniversary. In the soft candlelight, as my husband and I watch his parents embrace, I slip my hand into his, and he covers it with his own. It is their celebration, yet we rejoice in the heritage of love they pass on to us. And in their eyes we see the joyful affirmation of their lives: Best friends are valentines forever.

Pamela Kennedy is a freelance writer of short stories, articles, essays, and children's books. Wife of a naval officer and mother of three children, she has made her home on both U.S. coasts and currently resides in Honolulu, Hawaii. She draws her material from her own experiences and memories, adding highlights from her imagination to enhance the story.

Beauty Is Forever

Margaret Rorke

Beauty is forever
    If it lies beneath the skin.
Time can't reach to sever
    That which blossoms from within.

Cheeks may crack, revealing
    All the decades drifted by;
But there's no concealing
    What still sparkles in the eye.

When the ore is tested
    By the flames of love and trust,
Where it long has rested,
    It rebuts the surface rust.

There can be no fading
    Of a pattern wrapped by years
To withstand invading
    By a multitude of fears.

Beauty is forever,
    Given what should be its role.
Age is not so clever
    As to wrinkle up the soul.

My Grandmother's Love Letters

Hart Crane

There are no stars tonight
But those of memory.
Yet how much room for memory there is
In the loose girdle of soft rain.

There is even room enough
For the letters of my mother's mother,
Elizabeth,

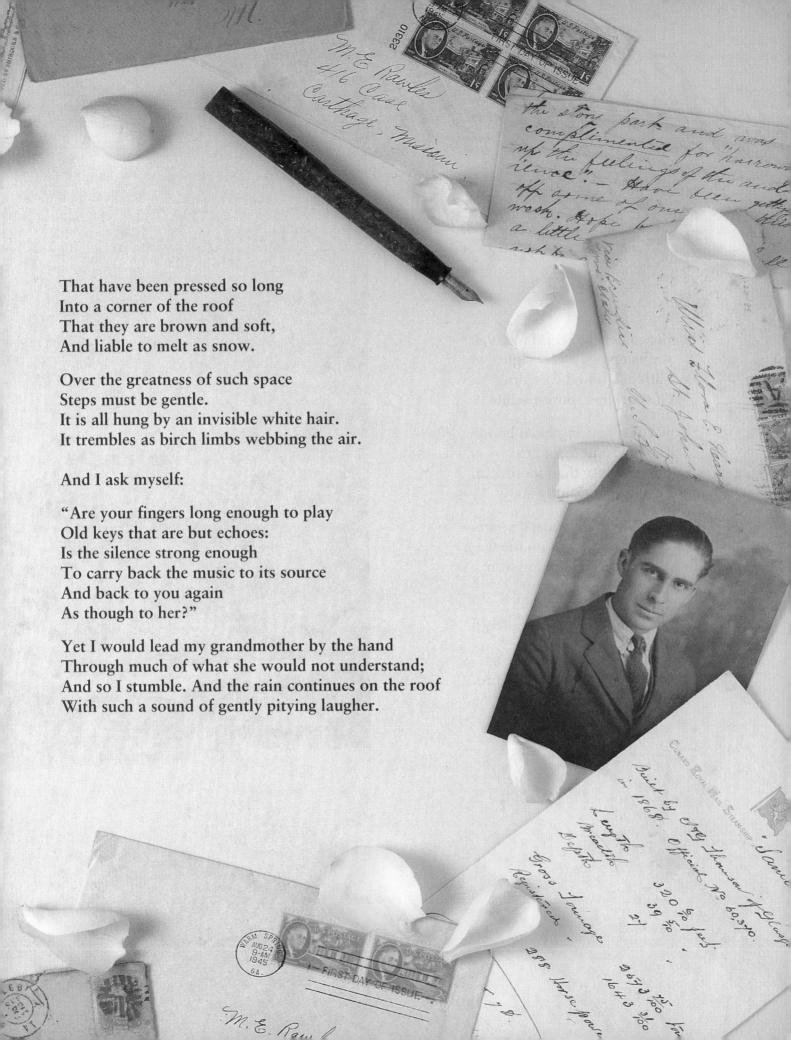

That have been pressed so long
Into a corner of the roof
That they are brown and soft,
And liable to melt as snow.

Over the greatness of such space
Steps must be gentle.
It is all hung by an invisible white hair.
It trembles as birch limbs webbing the air.

And I ask myself:

"Are your fingers long enough to play
Old keys that are but echoes:
Is the silence strong enough
To carry back the music to its source
And back to you again
As though to her?"

Yet I would lead my grandmother by the hand
Through much of what she would not understand;
And so I stumble. And the rain continues on the roof
With such a sound of gently pitying laugher.

Snowed-In Days

Georgia B. Adams

In silence lies the world today,
    A glistening, lovely sight
Beneath its quilted comforter
    Of sparkling, purest white.

Snow covers every naked bough;
    The birds flit to and fro
And almost lose their footing on
    The light and fluffy snow.

I look at yonder clouds; it seems
    That more snow's on the way;
I love to watch it slipping from
    A sky of pewter gray!

These snowed-in days are warm
        hearth days;
    And as the flames leap high,
I snuggle near the crackling fire
    And sigh a wistful sigh!

MOUNT MANSFIELD
Pleasant Valley, Vermont
Gene Ahrens Photography

Country CHRONICLE
─Lansing Christman─

BRIDGES

Nature builds a bridge to loving friendships which, in mid-February of each year, invariably result in many valentines in my mailbox. Through the love of nature that nurtures my soul, I have met others who share this same feeling. Thus, a bond of friendship has formed a lasting link of love between us, a link as firm and certain as the returning winter every year.

To lovers of nature, each season brings its own unique joys and treasures. In winter, it is the mood that my friends and I love—the smiles, songs, and quiet moments that fill this season of icy splendor. The majesty we see in winter never fails to bring a smile to our faces. We can see the beauty in each and every cold snowflake that falls from pewter-gray skies. We can see the beauty in rolling fields blanketed with fluffy, white comforters of fresh snow.

When my friends and I hear the lilting songs of the winter birds outside our windows, we feel our spirits lift and soar right along with those lovely melodies. Just the other day I enjoyed a veritable concert in my front yard when the songs of the bluebirds, the chickadees, and the cardinals mingled together.

I also love the hushed stillness of the outside world during a snowfall, a much rarer occurrence here in the Carolina hills compared to upstate New York where I grew up. I have always savored a short walk through the winter snow. Those are the quiet moments when I feel closest to my Maker. I know my friends savor their own quiet moments of winter solitude too.

All these winter treasures—the smiles, the songs, and the quiet moments—are true gifts of nature and become a part of special friendships. Love and nurture our natural world, this creation of God's, and a bridge will form. Over that bridge, valentines will come to you in the form of loving friends.

The author of two published books, Lansing Christman has been contributing to Ideals *for more than twenty years. Mr. Christman has also been published in several American, foreign, and braille anthologies. He lives in rural South Carolina.*

HUTCHINS BRIDGE
Montgomery Center, Vermont
Gene Ahrens Photography

OWACHOMO BRIDGE. Natural Bridges National Monument, Utah. John Elk III Photography.

NATURAL BRIDGES NATIONAL MONUMENT

The desert sun warms my shoulders as I gaze across the ruddy cliffs of Utah's Canyonlands region. As I lean over to tighten the lace on my hiking boot, a spiny red lizard dashes across the rocks. He pauses for a moment as if to ask why I have wandered into his desert homeland, and then he scampers away. With my boots laced properly and my water jug filled, I begin my descent into the golden canyon.

The turquoise sky makes a canopy over the sun-drenched cliffs of Natural Bridges National

64

Monument. Erosion and weather have created a natural staircase between the mesa top, where I begin, and the canyon floor. As I carefully pick my way over the uneven terrain, I notice the green fir trees, which seem oddly out of place among the rocks. It amazes me that so many plants and animals live in this rugged climate. On many summer afternoons, the temperature climbs above one hundred degrees Fahrenheit. But I have chosen a mild spring day for my excursion, and the air feels fresh with just a hint of coolness.

As I near a ledge, the first natural bridge comes into view. The slab of rock sweeps across the blue sky as if suspended in the air by magic. Such bridges form when a river curves severely (almost circling back on itself) and a thin wall of sandstone is created. Over time, floodwaters cause heavy erosion and eventually break through the sandstone wall. The "bridge" grows larger due to continued erosion.

The Canyonlands' Sipapu Bridge is the second largest natural bridge in the world. Discovered by a prospector in 1883, Sipapu and two other natural bridges were featured in *National Geographic Magazine* in 1904. Just four years later, President Theodore Roosevelt proclaimed the area a national monument. Sipapu Bridge and nearby Kachina and Owachomo Bridges were named for Hopi Indian words. At the time, the names seemed appropriate because cliff dwellings and artifacts found in the area resembled those of the Hopi. Archaeologists later learned that the dwellings actually belonged to the Anasazi Indians. These people inhabited southeastern Utah hundreds of years ago, where they farmed the mesas, wove baskets, and made pottery.

Farther down the trail, I catch a glimpse of an Anasazi village. Primitive dwellings and the ruins of a *kiva*, or ceremonial gathering place, hide among the cliffs. Viewing the ancient ruins, I try to imagine what it would have been like to carve my life out of the desert rock.

I wonder what the Mexican traders and Spanish explorers thought of this majestic landscape. These groups arrived in Utah during the mid 1700s, followed by fur trappers and pioneers. While Utah's crimson gorges and cliffs create a brilliant view for tourists, they must have presented a formidable obstacle to travelers pulling covered wagons.

Reaching Kachina Bridge, I stop to rest my feet and take a swig from my water bottle. I notice a pile of boulders nearby, evidence of a recent rock slide. Kachina Bridge, the youngest of the three natural bridges, is also the bulkiest. During the summer months, floodwaters continue to whittle away at this massive stone.

Tromping farther down the trail, I near the end of my journey. The last bridge, Owachomo, is also the most striking. A great arm of sandstone reaches across the canyon, creating a window of blue sky beneath it. I stop to marvel at the formation, which seems to defy gravity.

A cool breeze whispers through the gorge, and I realize the sun has dropped toward the horizon. Climbing out of the canyon, I stop to absorb the spectacular view. The blushing red buttes have turned a dusty shade of lavender. The blazing sunshine has given way, and I reach into my backpack for my long-sleeved shirt. Leaning against a rock, I sip my water and watch dusk come to the Canyonlands.

Next to me, a photographer sets up a tripod and positions her camera. Like her, I want to capture a piece of the sunset and take it home as a reminder of nature's tranquility and the beauty of the canyon. I know we are not the first people to have this wish. Perhaps an Anasazi girl or a pioneer woman from years ago took a mental snapshot of a similar sunset and tucked it away for later.

A native of Texas, Laura K. Griffis is finishing her senior year at Vanderbilt University while working as an Ideals *editorial intern. Laura collects postcards from her travels to museums around the world as a part of her ongoing study of international cultures.*

THE HANDS OF TIME. Superstock.

Endless Love

Harold F. Mohn

I cannot stop the hands of time
Much as I'd like to do,
But neither can I stop the love
Within my heart for you.

I cannot stop the rolling waves
As they beat on the shore,
But neither can I stop the love
That lives forevermore.

I cannot change what lies ahead,
Though good or bad it be,
But neither can I change my love
That lives eternally.

I would not change a single thing
Since that day I met you,
Because the love within my heart
Grows more each day anew.

WINTER BUNDLE. Superstock.

Snow Wishes

LaVerne P. Larson

On early winter mornings
    When the sky wore darkest gray,
I remember as a child
    How I would wish for snow that day.

I'd dress and eat my breakfast,
    And then off to school I'd run
While dreaming of a world in white
    That held such magic fun.

TUNNEL OF FUN. Superstock.

My heart would stray so often
    Through the frosty panes of glass,
Wishing with a child's faith
    To see the snowflakes pass.

The school day seemed quite endless;
    But as the last bell pealed,
A miracle had visited
    Each treetop, street, and field.

The snowflakes swirled and danced with glee
    And kissed me on the cheek;
My feet flew home as if with wings,
    My sled and skates to seek.

Then out I'd go for happy times
    Into a world of white
To play with friends who shared my joy
    At such a wondrous sight.

We'd slide and skate and snowmen make,
    Build forts, make snowballs fly;
Those hours were such joyous ones
    Beneath the winter sky.

Too soon the twilight closed my day
    And homeward I would go
To dream that night of future fun
    Within my world of snow.

Ideals' Family Recipes

Favorite Recipes from the Ideals Family of Readers

Editor's Note: Please send us your best-loved recipes! Mail a typed copy of the recipe along with your name, address, and telephone number to Ideals magazine, ATTN: Recipes, P.O. Box 305300, Nashville, Tennessee 37230. We will pay $10 for each recipe used. Recipes cannot be returned.

SAVORY BEEF STEW WITH DILLY DUMPLINGS

In a small bowl, combine ½ cup all-purpose flour, 1 teaspoon salt, and ¼ teaspoon pepper. Cut 2 pounds lean beef chuck roast into 1½-inch cubes. Coat cubes with flour mixture. In a Dutch oven, heat 3 tablespoons vegetable oil. Add beef and remaining flour mixture; sauté until beef is brown on all sides. Add 4 cups water and heat until boiling. Reduce heat, cover, and simmer 1½ hours. Add 1 bay leaf; 2 tablespoons snipped parsley; ½ teaspoon dried thyme; 1½ cups thinly sliced carrots; 1 cup thinly sliced celery; 2 sliced, medium onions; and 4 cups potatoes cut in ¾-inch cubes. Stir. Cover and simmer an additional 30 minutes.

In a small bowl, sift together 1½ cups all-purpose flour, 2 teaspoons baking powder, ¼ teaspoon dried parsley flakes, ¼ teaspoon ground thyme, ¼ teaspoon dried dillweed, and ½ teaspoon salt. Set aside. In a medium bowl, combine 2 tablespoons oil, ⅔ cup milk, and 1 egg, slightly beaten. Add flour mixture and stir just until blended. Drop batter by spoonfuls onto hot beef or vegetables (do not drop directly into liquid). Cook uncovered 10 minutes over low heat. Cover and cook an additional 10 minutes. Makes 6 to 8 servings.

Bernadine Dirmeyer
Harpster, Ohio

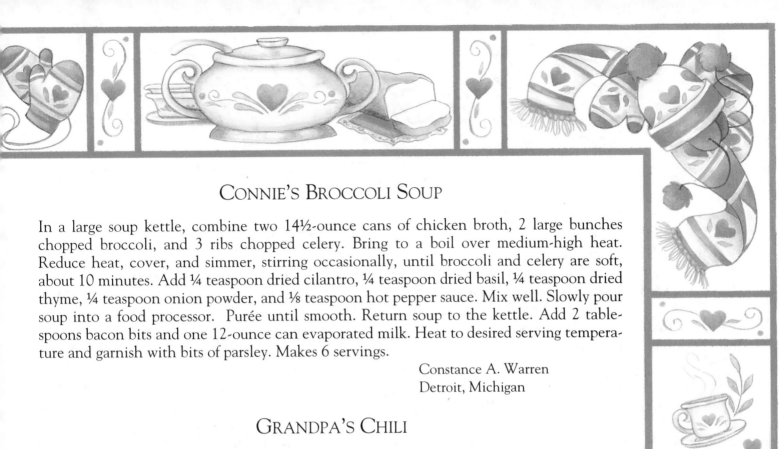

CONNIE'S BROCCOLI SOUP

In a large soup kettle, combine two 14½-ounce cans of chicken broth, 2 large bunches chopped broccoli, and 3 ribs chopped celery. Bring to a boil over medium-high heat. Reduce heat, cover, and simmer, stirring occasionally, until broccoli and celery are soft, about 10 minutes. Add ¼ teaspoon dried cilantro, ¼ teaspoon dried basil, ¼ teaspoon dried thyme, ¼ teaspoon onion powder, and ⅛ teaspoon hot pepper sauce. Mix well. Slowly pour soup into a food processor. Purée until smooth. Return soup to the kettle. Add 2 tablespoons bacon bits and one 12-ounce can evaporated milk. Heat to desired serving temperature and garnish with bits of parsley. Makes 6 servings.

Constance A. Warren
Detroit, Michigan

GRANDPA'S CHILI

In a large skillet, heat 6 tablespoons vegetable oil. Add 2 finely chopped onions and 4 finely chopped garlic cloves; sauté until golden. Add 2 pounds ground beef or turkey and sauté until brown. Transfer mixture to a Dutch oven. Add 4 cups water, 2 chopped green peppers, 1 teaspoon celery seed, ½ teaspoon cayenne, 2 teaspoons crushed cumin, 2 small bay leaves, 4 tablespoons chili powder, ¼ teaspoon basil, 1 teaspoon salt, and two 16-ounce cans crushed tomatoes. Stir until well blended. Bring chili to a boil and simmer uncovered for at least 3 hours or to desired consistency. One hour before serving, add two 15-ounce cans of kidney beans. Makes 8 to 12 servings.

Wendy Swope
Victor, Idaho

GRANDMOTHER'S HEARTY HAMBURGER SOUP

In a 4-quart saucepan, bring 7 cups of water to a boil; add 2 beef bouillon cubes and ½ cup barley. Mix well. Cover and simmer covered for 45 to 50 minutes or until barley is soft. In a large skillet, sauté 1 pound ground beef with ½ cup chopped onion and 1 clove minced garlic until meat is cooked and onion is soft. Drain well and set aside. When the barley is thoroughly cooked, add meat mixture, one 8-ounce can tomato sauce, 1 cup water, ½ cup sliced carrots, one 10-ounce can corn (drained), 1 cup cut cabbage, ¼ cup chopped green pepper, 1 teaspoon dillweed, and salt and pepper to taste. Simmer an additional 45 minutes. Makes 8 servings.

Carolyn E. Fritz
North Royalton, Ohio

OUR POND
Carolyn Bakken

In the rolling hills of Minnesota where I grew up, Valentine's Day usually brought another thick coating of pure white snow. The pond that lay sleeping in the hollow just below our big, white farmhouse pulled its blanket of ice thickly and securely over the lethargic water. My window overlooked the frozen winter wonderland that seemed to whisper, "Come! Bring your skates. It has been too long since your silver blades glided over me."

Because I was younger than my brothers, I had to wait each winter until they tested the ice. When my father said it was frozen solid, we took our skates off the nails in the basement, threw them over our shoulders like professionals, climbed over the barbed wire fence that kept the cows from getting into our yard, and trudged down the snow-laden hill to the pond.

My fingers burned with cold as I laced up my skates and took my first wobbly step out on the frozen ice. When I was much smaller, I first pushed a wooden, folding chair around the ice for security, kind of like riding a bicycle with training wheels. After learning how to maneuver, I left my wooden chair on the pond's edge for a weary skater. Soon my ankles stopped careening and the blades stood erect and confident. I pushed my way out onto the ice and glided from one side to the other, the wind biting and tickling at my reddened cheeks. How quickly my confidence returned! When I was asked to play crack-the-whip with the neighborhood children who also skated on our pond, I even took the dreaded position at the end of the long, snakelike line.

If tiny ripples formed on our pond when it froze, my brothers chopped a hole through the ice and flooded the pond to make the skating smoother. My brothers and their friends hauled buckets of water from the hole in the ice up to the top of the hill that ran down to the pond. The races soon began to see whose spilled pail of water would run the farthest before it froze in the below-zero weather. We really didn't care who won because the hill became a slick, fast, icy run for our sleds and toboggans. Now the concern was whose sled could go the farthest out onto the pond. I never won, but it sure was fun.

My father, knowing the night temperatures often dropped below zero, hauled old rubber tires down to the pond's edge. Soon a blazing fire warmed the shores of our pond so the night skaters could warm up before once again joining the frivolity on the ice. Father sank an upright pole into the ice and extended a much longer pole on a pivot. We tied a sled to the extended pole, and it became a merry-go-round of sorts. We took turns pushing the pole around on its pivot while the rider on the end clung tightly to the sled. When the speed was too great and he sailed off the sled onto the smooth ice, there was always another child eagerly awaiting his or her turn.

Of course, the winter playground enticed all the neighborhood children. Bundled in warm winter jackets with lots of colorful mittens and mufflers knitted by grandmas, the pond resembled a brilliant array of fall leaves. But the best part came when, after an afternoon of frisky frolicking, we weary skaters once again trudged up the hill, seemingly so much farther this time, to the big, warm kitchen and the relished heat of the wood stove. Leaving little puddles on the worn linoleum floor, we peeled off layers and layers of clothing. But when the tedious task was over, steaming mugs of hot chocolate stood as our prize on the kitchen table. And on Valentine's Day, our hot chocolate was usually accompanied by tasty cakes and cookies. The heat of the hot chocolate warmed our frosted fingers and sent waves of warmth through our chilled bodies while the sweets gave our taste buds a treat. The next day, if the weather permitted, we would once more don the layers of coats, scarves, and mittens and step out into our winter wonderland again.

Winter Warmth

Mary A. Barnard

There is something rather cozy
About a winter day
When all around is snow and ice
That won't soon melt away.

The earth is wrapped in garments white,
And fence posts one by one
Will become a studded pillar
That glistens in the sun.

While each tree is hung with pendants
Like crystal jewels rare
And the view from every window
Is grand beyond compare,

Inside the fire burns merrily;
The hearthside sends out cheer,
Enjoying home and family
This cozy time of year.

WINTER RETREAT
Ketchum, Idaho
Dick Dietrich Photography

From My Garden Journal

by Deana Deck

CROCUS

"I haven't seen a crocus or a rosebud,
Or a robin on the wing,
But I feel so gay, in a melancholy way,
That it might as well be spring."

That song, from the 1940s version of the movie *State Fair*, led to a family joke retold at every reunion since I was a child. I had just turned seven when I saw the movie; and not being much of a gardener at that tender age, I was unfamiliar with the word *crocus*. Behind their farmhouse, my grandparents had a deep cistern in which they kept frogs for fish bait. At some point that summer I asked my grandmother if I could go play with the crocus. After much questioning, she finally determined that I was referring to the frogs.

"That's what they're called," I said. "Crocus."

"You mean croaker," she replied.

"No," I assured her. "A croaker is one frog. A crocus is a bunch of them." And so I entered the family Hall of Malapropism Fame.

One reason I was unfamiliar with this cheerful little spring plant is that we moved so often as a military family that it was futile to plant bulbs or perennials. Consequently, I was grown and out on my own before I ever became aware of these delightful harbingers of springtime.

For years, gardens have been blooming with drifts of blue or golden yellow crocuses; but now, thanks to hybridizers, a multitude of colors is available. Many crocus species exist; some are early bloomers, some bloom in later spring, and some even bloom in autumn. Oddly enough, these early spring flowering bulbs, which actually grow from corms (which are similar to bulbs but do not have scales), are members of the iris family. The normal blooming period for a crocus is from two to four weeks, but by selecting a variety of species, you can enjoy beautiful crocus blooms for three to four months.

Crocus verna, the common crocus, is the species most frequently grown in the United States. Its petals are usually either lilac or white and often streaked with purple. It is among the group of hardier crocuses and can withstand winter temperatures as low as -30° F. For southern gardens, the Greek *Crocus siberi* and the Italian *Crocus imperati* are preferred since they will often bloom in midwinter and will not be harmed by hot summers. A variety which blooms in mid March is the brilliant yellow Cloth of Gold, *Crocus agustifolius*. This hardy variety is an excellent choice for most temperate climates.

Bright yellow is a cheery sight in spring, but it can become tiresome in fall. If you'd like something to contrast with the ubiquitous yellows and oranges of autumn, add a drift of rose, lilac, blue, or purple crocuses to the landscape. Several species bloom in autumn. September brings the light blue, large blooms of *Crocus speciosus*; the lilac and white Saffron crocus (whose stigma is used as an herb and food coloring); and the bright lilac *Crocus pulchellus*. One variety of pulchellus, Zephyr, produces white blooms. As late as mid October, the *Crocus asturicus* displays its blooms. Another autumn bloomer is the beautiful *Crocus ochroleucus*, which has white blooms tinted with creamy apricot on the outside and orange inner surfaces. It's the exact color of a Creamsicle!

By combining the earliest bloomers, which will appear when snow is still on the ground, with a few later varieties, you can have beautiful crocus blooms throughout the spring. Then in autumn, the same area can bloom again with fall varieties.

Crocuses are easy to grow and can be naturalized anywhere. One plant alone may look rather forlorn because crocuses are so tiny and sit so low in the landscape, so plant them in groups of six or more about four inches deep. They look wonderful in rock gardens, under trees, and even scattered throughout the lawn. Just don't plan to begin mowing the grass early! Crocuses need to remain uncut until their grasslike foliage has died back; cutting the foliage prematurely is the greatest cause of failure. Actually, it's perhaps the second greatest cause since squirrels probably rate higher on the list; crocus corms are one of their favorite foods. You can protect the bulbs from hungry vermin by placing chicken wire over the bed and carefully pinning the edges with wire.

Depending on your area, it is usually best to plant spring-blooming crocuses around September and fall-blooming crocuses in the early sum-

One plant alone may look rather forlorn because crocuses are so tiny and sit so low in the landscape, so plant them in groups of six or more about four inches deep.

mer. When planted in good soil with plenty of sunlight, the plants will reward you by multiplying rapidly, both by dropping seed and by developing cormlets. As the crocuses mature and divide, you can dig and separate them for replanting.

Crocuses do best when planted in drifts in full sun. You can extend the life of your crocus bed by planting the early-blooming varieties in a protected location with soil that warms early. They will bloom up to two weeks earlier than normal under these conditions.

Crocuses also do very well indoors as forced plants. Set a dozen or more into a shallow bulb pan filled with loose potting mixture. These are one of the few bulb plants that can be forced and later moved into the garden for repeat blooming in following years. If you decide to force the bulbs, or corms, it is important that you store them at near-freezing temperatures in your refrigerator until time to plant.

It may take a little sleuthing on your part to find the garden centers and catalogs that offer some of the less common varieties of crocuses, but believe me, it is well worth it. Especially when you peep out your frosty window on those chilly mornings in January, February, or March to see brightly colored waves of happy blossoms basking in the sunshine as a promise that spring, robins, and even croaking frogs will soon be arriving.

Deana Deck lives in Nashville, Tennessee, where her popular garden column is a regular feature in The Tennessean.

Readers' Forum
Meet Our Ideals Readers and Their Families

ATTENTION *IDEALS* READERS: The *Ideals* editors are looking for "favorite holiday memories" for the magazine. Please send a typed description of your favorite holiday memory to: Favorite Memories, c/o Editorial Department, Ideals Publications Inc., P.O. Box 305300, Nashville, Tennessee 37230.

REBECCA CHILDRESS snapped this photo when her two-year-old grandson Dylan Dugan was visiting her at her chicken farm in Ranger, Georgia. Rebecca proudly tells us that Dylan is one of thirteen grandchildren. Dylan traveled to Georgia from California where his father was stationed in the service. At his grandparents' house, Dylan was fascinated with the chicken house. Rebecca tells us he also loved playing with the neighbor's pig, Grunt. Grunt even wandered over to see Dylan every day!

Rebecca says she greatly enjoys her collection of *Ideals*; some of her favorite *Ideals* date as far back as 1947.

STEVE AND ROBERTA VALDEZ of Elko, Nevada, sent us this photo of Samantha, an orphan calf who was born last spring. Samantha enjoyed resting by the dog house at the Valdezes home at Maggie Creek Ranch. Steve and Roberta's three children also live out West, two in Utah and one in Idaho. The Valdezes have four grandchildren.

One of Roberta's favorite hobbies is reading, and she has been reading *Ideals* since her neighbor showed her a copy of our magazine eight years ago.

SYLVIA SATTLER of Bertrand, Nebraska, says her grandson Addison is just one of a whole "wheelbarrow full" of grandchildren she and her husband John adore. The couple celebrate their fortieth wedding anniversary this year, just a week before Valentine's Day. They have seven children and nine grandchildren. Addison (picture here) and little sister Elise are the children of Gina and Corby Jensen who also live in Nebraska.

When she is not photographing her grandchildren, Sylvia likes to cook, sew, and do needlework. She also collects *Ideals* magazines, which she has enjoyed since she began reading them at her mother's house years ago. Happy anniversary Sylvia and John!

ROSY WILLIAMSON of Minneapolis, Minnesota, often uses *Ideals* to help her create displays in the nursing home where she works. She crafted this delightful schoolroom collage using *Ideals* magazines. Rosy says the schoolroom pictured here brings back happy memories of the one-room schoolhouse she attended in 1957.

THANK YOU Rebecca Childress, Steve and Roberta Valdez, Sylvia Sattler, and Rosy Williamson for sharing with *Ideals*. We hope to hear from other readers who would like to share photos and stories with the *Ideals* family. Include a self-addressed, stamped envelope if you would like the photos returned. Keep your original photographs for safekeeping and send duplicate photos along with your name, address, and telephone number to:

READERS' FORUM
IDEALS PUBLICATIONS INC.
P.O. BOX 305300
NASHVILLE, TENNESSEE
37230

ideals

Publisher, Patricia A. Pingry
Editor, Lisa C. Ragan
Copy Editor, Michelle Prater Burke
Electronic Prepress Manager, Amilyn K. Lanning
Editorial Intern, Laura K. Griffis
Contributing Editors, Lansing Christman, Deana Deck, Russ Flint, Pamela Kennedy, Patrick McRae, Mary Skarmeas, Nancy Skarmeas

ACKNOWLEDGMENTS
MY GRANDMOTHER'S LOVE LETTERS was excerpted from *COMPLETE POEMS OF HART CRANE* by Hart Crane, with permission of the publisher, Liveright Publishing Corporation. Copyright © 1933, 1958, 1966 by Liveright Publishing Corporation. Copyright © 1986 by Marc Simon. PUP IN A SNOWSTORM by Frances Frost, copyright © 1944 by *THE SATURDAY EVENING POST*. TO A LITTLE GIRL from *HARBOR LIGHTS OF HOME* by Edgar A. Guest, copyright © 1928 by The Reilly & Lee Co. Used by permission of the author's estate. Excerpt from RENASCENCE from *COLLECTED POEMS* by Edna St. Vincent Millay, HarperCollins. Copyright © 1912, 1940 by Edna St. Vincent Millay.

Sing Me a Song of Love

Viola Jacobson Berg

Sing me a song of a golden sky,
Of stars and comets blazing by.
Sing me a song with a dream and a sigh;
  Sing me a song of love.

Sing me a song of daffodils,
Of nesting birds and peaceful hills,
Of waking spring when nature thrills;
  Sing me a song of love.

Sing me a song of joys and tears
Where happy notes drown out the fears
And the melody lasts a million years;
  Sing me a song of love.

Statement of ownership, management, and circulation (Required by 39 U.S.C. 3685), of Ideals, published eight times a year in February, March, May, June, August, September, November, and December at Nashville, Tennessee, for September 1995. Publisher, Patricia A. Pingry; Editor, Lisa C. Ragan; Managing Editor, as above; Owner, Ideals Publications Incorporated, 535 Metroplex Drive, Suite 250, Nashville, Tennessee 37211. Stockholders: Simon Waterlow, President; Martin Flanagan, Vice President; Patricia A. Pingry, Vice President, 535 Metroplex Drive, Suite 250, Nashville, Tennessee 37211. Known bondholders, mortgages, and other security holders: Egmont Foundation, VOGNMAGERGADE II, 1148 Copenhagen K., Denmark and Trans Financial Bank, P.O. Box 3490, Clarksville, Tennessee 37043. Average no. copies each issue during preceding 12 months: Total no. copies printed (Net Press Run) 200,775. Paid circulation 38,197. Mail subscription 152,942. Total paid circulation 191,139. Free distribution 357. Total distribution 200,775. Actual no. copies of single issue published nearest to filing date: Total no. copies printed (Net Press Run) 168,607. Paid circulation 7,363. Mail subscription 143,027. Total paid circulation 150,390. Free distribution 235. Total distribution 150,625. I certify that the statements made by me above are correct and complete. Rose A. Yates, Vice President, Direct Marketing Systems and Operations.